D0822122

This book belongs to:

_____

a Superhero

SUPERHEROES WEAR MASKS!

Kathy Patten
Illustrated by Mary Patten Priestley

DEDICATED TO
ALL HELPERS -
EVERYWHERE.

Superheroes we see
on screen and in books,
But those all around us
let's not overlook.

Helpers are our real
superheroes, we know,
clad in their masks,
off working they go!

Off to a fire
in a building tall,
then rescue a kitty
before a fall.

There goes a police car
speeding by,
Someone needs help –
too bad it can't fly.

Yes it was going
as fast as a race,
but you could still see
a mask on each face!

Wow! Where are
they going?

Here comes an ambulance
with all its lights flashing.
Off to the hospital
it soon will be dashing.

The driver and
all of the medic crew
will make sure their
masks are on tight, too!

In the hospital and offices
are doctors and nurses
Ready to help anyone
who needs their services.

They give check-ups
and shots to make us well.
Nice smiles under their masks –
you can always tell!

Bye-Bye!

Loaded full,
a city bus quietly coasts
It's fun to spot
the big purple ones most!

Wearing a mask,
the driver tall in her seat
with riders glad
to get out of the heat.

Now off to the grocery –
our cupboards are low.
Busy clerks work hard
so we'll have food when we go.

The nice baker has sprinkled cookies so sweet! With milk, who could resist that yummy treat?

Before too long, we will go
back to school,
to meet the teacher,
see friends – how cool!

It will be a new adventure –
I'll tell you why,
We'll be wearing masks to class,
but don't be shy!

All these nice helpers,
superheroes they are,
they keep us well and safe,
they're real stars!
But they need
all of our help each day –
and we can do it
in a very big way.

How can I help?

In our kingdom,
and the ones far away,
Lives a mean germ
and that is not okay!

That nasty germ tries
to make everyone sick,
But with our masks
we give it a great big kick!

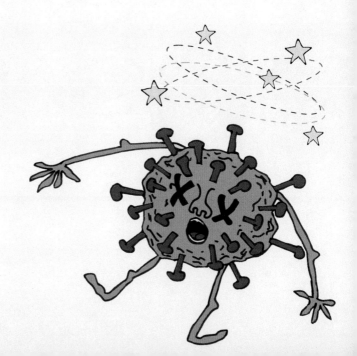

The doctors and nurses
and all who are wise,
want us to wear a mask
made in just our size.

One day, the mean germ
will finally be gone,
but until then,
our masks have to stay on!

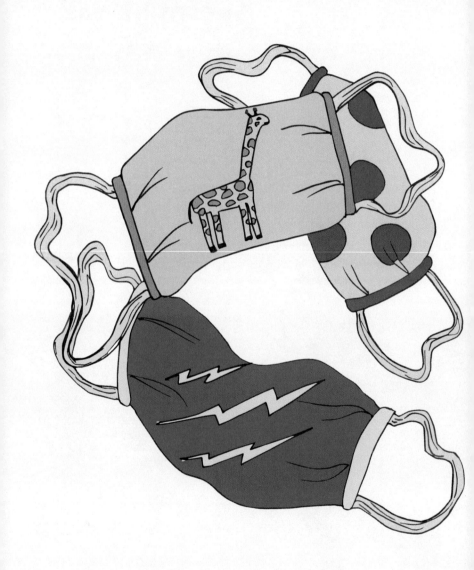

A mask might have
polka-dots,
or a cute giraffe,
and we will smile
when it helps
someone laugh.

Helpers,
superheroes,
whatever the name
Wearing our masks
we can be
one of the same!

Superheroes we see
on screen and in books,
But those all around us
let's not overlook.

Helpers are our real
superheroes, we know,
clad in their masks,
off working they go!

You're a Superhero, too!

Made in the USA
Middletown, DE
18 January 2021

31862689R00020